Air Fryer Recipe Book

Practical Air Fryer Recipes for Beginners Plus Innovative Users

Jenny Mayers

Contents

INTRODUCTION

Many people would have liked fried food but they knew it was bad because of its high-fat content. Frying is doable without needing oil, correct? Yes, oil-free and low-fat fried food may be delicious.

The modern air fryer uses hot air to cook without using any oil. That doesn't make sense. Grandma would say that the dish would be flavorless and dry. That wonderful crunch on the exterior, moist and soft on the inside has always been accomplished through deep-frying in a huge amount of oil.

Hot air cooks like a rotisserie, so the food's exterior stays crisp and the interior remains moist. These healthy fryers use heated air for cooking the food. Due to the machine's compact size, the high heat seals in the food fluids get the food to cook quickly. Between 1.8 to below 4 pounds cooking capacity is the norm for the market's popular hot air frying devices.

Food is placed on the cooking basket and receives the intense flow of hot air blowing in all directions. This keeps the food evenly cooked. Frying only requires a teaspoon of oil, which causes less calorie intake.

A single machine may be utilized for most of your cooking needs, thanks to the air fryer's great versatility. Whether you're cooking fresh food or frozen food, you can cook nearly all types of dishes in the fryer. Almost all meals may be prepared in less than 30 minutes if cooked quickly.

Moms who are often juggling their schedules would adore the air fryer for all of the reasons listed above. Their kids' meals were prepared with only the smallest effort and a short amount of time. Air fryers would be advantageous to college students too, as they are quite adaptable and relatively simple to clean up. No oily residue is left behind.

People over the age of sixty would find the air fryer to be very easy to use. Everything to adjust is done with only two buttons: temperature and timer. A healthy cuisine that does not contain oil would be excellent for their health.

Low-fat dieters, especially those on keto, would also appreciate the deep fryer, as it uses a fat-free or less-oil cooking approach. You'll have greater control over what you eat because you can eat your favorite comfort meal in a more nutritious way.
To find out more about the advantages of using a hot air fryer, read this short guide on healthy cooking using Air fryers.

Let's get started!

CHAPTER 1
What Is Air Fryer?

Would you like food prepared by air frying? If so, please continue reading. A new cooking technology that uses hot air to fry, roast or grill food without requiring large amounts of oil or fat has been developed.

If I cut off the generous usage of oil, how does it taste?
The truth is that the cooking process incorporates both the texture and taste of deep-fried meals. If you can give up using oil, you will be helping yourself stay healthy by reducing your risk of cardiovascular disease.

Before the purchase of the microwaves and slow cookers during the 1970s, the hot air frying machines introduced to the kitchen were the only other major piece of equipment to revolutionize the function of the kitchen.

Because of the design of the appliances, hot air circulates throughout the appliance with much the same effect as the flow and movement of heat currents within a pot filled with boiling oil.

Thus, the technique helps to make the dish crunchy on the exterior while the inside cooks. In certain contemporary designs, grilling features are incorporated into the design to improve crispness and better browning.

Air frying has been developed to be utilized for oil-less healthy cooking. The dish is juicy and tender on the inside with crispy, brown skin on the exterior.

Deep-fat frying VS Air-frying
First, there is a very mild difference in taste between the two. The enthusiasts who enjoy the air-fried items have greatly outnumbered those who believe deep-fried items are tastier.

It's also the truth that, when you eat air-fried food, the nauseating oil flavor that constantly gets to your stomach is completely absent. For the most part, the taste is pretty similar to deep-fried.

However, air-fried uses benefit lesser labor, less oil odor in the house and simplified cleanup. With this, you don't have to feel sick from eating lots of fried food, which means you may enjoy that kind of food more regularly.

One absolute absence of difficulties thanks to the elimination of air frying. However, on the surface, the air fryer method seems to be more time-consuming than deep frying.

Compared to deep-frying, airfrying takes 25 minutes while it takes only 8 minutes for the deep-frying approach. Though air frying takes less time in terms of energy use and total cooking time, it uses more energy overall.

As far as I'm concerned, pre-and post-deep-frying warm-up/cool-down duration and all the other extra steps are included in the total time. Air frying saves you the time for the oil to heat up, time for the oil to cool down, time for cleaning, time for filtering and storage for oil just to name a few.

Strengths

Foods on the menu that you like will be served again. People have been advising you not to eat most junk meals since the content of these foods is not that important. Instead, these meals yield after preparation are the main cause of these meals being avoided. Nutritionists will recommend the same food that they told you not to consume when you air-fry it.

For this frying, the natural fats and oils are appropriate. Additionally, you can load your dish with avocado oil, walnut oil, grape seed oil, among others, to provide an oily texture and appearance. The only type of cooking oil used for hot air frying is healthy gourmet cooking oil.

When using this strategy, the frying troubles are substantially minimized or eliminated.

Economical air frying is possible. Because of the high cost of cooking oils and fats, especially when deep-frying is involved, you end up paying a lot. Think of a scenario where you enjoy sweet cuisine but in the end, you save a great deal of cooking oil that you would have otherwise spent.

Other than all these great advantages, hot air frying is also considerably safer. The annual death toll caused by deep fat frying is approximately 1,000. Air frying can erase all of these Teens within the house can handle the air fryers simply and effortlessly. If you're concerned about the well-being of your body, along with the economy, health and convenience, air frying is the way to go.

CHAPTER 2
Benefits Of Using Air Fryer

Air frying is the new kid on the block that has recently found favor with most Western countries. Overweight's harmful effects have been linked to the increased consumption of oily food, which has inspired imaginative minds to engage in constant revolution.

Think of your regular fry and instead of dipping it in oil, simply sprinkle it with oil and place it into some type of food preparation machinery, which is adjusted to your specifications.

People are praising the usage of Air fryers in America, as this will allow them to enjoy oil-filled junk food without the negative health consequences. The air fryers are known for having included a free bag of food, which boosts their appeal in the market.

All of these wonderful offerings include:

- The amount of oil used is far smaller. Hence they are also inexpensive.
- Scientifically tested and using heated air, the Air fryers exploit the theory of air frying.
- Air fryers decrease the possibility of an oil leak, resulting in less oil on the kitchen surface.

- Deep-fried food may not taste the same as air-fried food but you will know when you've got it right since it will be the perfect taste.
- Cooking devices using the air fryer method have a scientific explanation and some models don't even require food to be turned because they accomplish the task automatically.
- Air-fried food is lower in calories and fat than other fried food. Many people believe this is the case for this reason, so they are not seen to pose any health risks.

Can deep-fried meals ever be healthy?

New air fryers have made the idea of eating healthy easier to accomplish. Although the new breed of Air fryers, like the Phillips and the Tefal, can be innovative in their fries, current models like the Actifry and the Philips may be trusted.

The vast majority of the time, what is intriguing is what the fryers' air fryers come with. It's about the same in terms of flavor. However, some debate among individuals who prefer deep-fried foods on whether or not Air-fried foods may taste like deep-fried foods.

You may use air fryers for cooking the same type of food that most consumers want deep-fried. Deep-frying typical fries and chips now use Air frying, for instance.

No detail, no matter how minute, is too small to be overlooked. Due to this, much respect is being given to the idea of using less oil or not using oil in food preparation—air-fried food for those who haven't.

It's quite simple to get fresh salads, sandwiches and healthful meals if you'd want but it can be challenging for many of us. For some who have lived their whole lives consuming deep-fried foods, the prospect of no longer able to consume favorite chicken wings or cherished French fries is a nightmare.

While some people may still desire deep-fried foods even when they try to lead a better lifestyle, new developments are available to meet this demand, such as the air fryer.

French Fries

Like most appliances in the kitchen, the air fryer has one difference: instead of using electricity, it uses hot air to cook food. Rather than cooking food with oil in a typical manner, the fryer uses hot air that may reach roughly 200 degrees Celsius to cook the meal. Recent iterations of the fryer have a feature that allows the temperature to be adjusted to ensure equal and accurate frying.

The air fryer is an advantage because it helps to make the food you prepare healthier. By eliminating the use of oil in the cooking process, you help keep the fat % of the dish to a minimum. In conventional fryers, the amount of oil used raises the saturated fat content and for some people, this has the additional effect of increasing the amount of fat in their food.

Most current air fryers have an exhaust system in place which helps to filter out the extra air. It is eco-friendly since it is cleaned, resulting in it being a safe and healthy environment.

A major advantage of utilizing an air fryer is that since air is used for cooking food, you may prepare meals without worrying about overcooking. Some cuts of meat need extra cooking time to be properly cooked. Not only may the price be a concern but so maybe the availability of various models in the market today.

Be sure to investigate the characteristics of the fryer you are considering purchasing. A factor that influences price is the level of equipment features. Therefore, certain models may be cheaper than others.

In addition to features such as an automatic timer, a touch screen surface for easier navigation or an integrated dial, you should search for other qualities that will assist you with your daily life.

Some devices are great at cooking huge quantities of food while others do not. Choose a big enough machine to handle a large group if you always plan to have a huge gathering.

CHAPTER 3
Using An Air Fryer To Cook

Using an air fryer instead of a deep-fryer is a healthy alternative to deep-frying. Instead of using boiling oil, hot air fryers use heated air for cooking food. Rapid Air Technology is the greatest air fryer technology for home usage since it is faster than other cooking technologies and reduces the amount of oil required to cook your food.

A hot air fryer is a cooking device that utilizes hot air. Cooking with only warm air doesn't make sense. More precisely, we are stating that it is swiftly moving hot air rather than just moving air heated swiftly. This trendy kitchen gadget has a heating element and a fan already installed.

To help keep the confined air inside the machine warm, the heating element heats the air and the fan blows the warm air around. This swiftly moving air cooks the food as it contacts it from all directions.

It does indeed appear to cook with hot air like a convection oven.

There are two kinds of air fryers in the market: one employs a cooking basket and the other doesn't.

To help answer this question, let's take a look at the best air fryer for home use.

The Philips hot air fryer is a well-known hot air cooker that utilizes the frying basket. 2 versions of the hot air cooker are currently available in the United States: the manual HD9220/26 and the digital HD9230/26.

However, the digital variant is equipped with a maximum timer of 60 minutes. It only has a 30-minute timer with manual air frying. It is straightforward to run. When food is placed in the basket which sits on a drip pan, the cooking process is started.

To ensure that food is cooked evenly, shaking the pan midway through the cooking process is recommended.

At the moment, just one brand of the paddle air fryer is available. A paddle on the Actifry stirs the food as it cooks. Without this, you would have to jiggle the meal during the cooking process.

You don't need to add any more oil to store-bought frozen food. Crispy and moist fries, for example, don't need to be added to any oil before cooking. Fried potatoes are a great snack when you're trying to watch your carbohydrate intake.

When cooking homemade fries, you should soak them in water for approximately half an hour and add around a tablespoon of oil before frying. The fries will have a similar texture to those fried in a huge amount of oil because of this action.

Yes, you can eat fried food and lose fat at the same time. It means that less oil, fewer calories and better-for-you food will be consumed.

CHAPTER 4

Is A Low-Fat Air Fryer Truly Capable Of Producing Crisp Chips?

Low-fat air fryers, such as the Tefal Actifry or the Philips Air Fryer, are most popular because of their great deep-fried chip options but with virtually no oil. If you're attempting to shed pounds, these devices must be really attractive.

When someone asks you whether you can only cook chips, you can answer with at least two possible answers. If you are willing to believe in the chip's authenticity, you can say "they truly taste like the deep-fried variety," which is true.

Essentially, both the two specific machines stated function as hot air circulating fans around the food that speeds up the cooking process in many cases. While the Tefal employs a paddle that pushes and spins the food inside the pan, the paddle of the Zyliss doesn't make direct contact with the food.

Concerning some meals, you must shake the pan halfway through the cooking period with the Philips, as it doesn't do this. Yes, you can cook a tremendous amount more with your air fryer. What you can prepare will depend on the model since they are designed differently.

With the Tefal, you don't have to do anything until the machine "sounds" to let you know when your food is done. It is important to shake the basket halfway through the cooking period if you are cooking something that needs this.

Coming back to the chip quality

With each of these models, you will end up with the same final product. Although they are not deep-fried, the point I'm making is not to argue that they don't look and taste excellent.

But for the most part, consumers agree that they are closest to the original and considerably better than oven chips made with low-fat content. If you prepare your potatoes, do you have to do anything differently?

To get the best results, you can use fresh chips instead of frozen ones but all you have to do is chip your potatoes like you normally would. Fast-cooking thin French fries only require about 10 minutes to prepare.

The best way to remove the starch from the chips is to soak them in water for at least half an hour and pat them dry before drizzling a couple of tablespoons of oil over the top. Prepare the fryer for use by heating it for a couple of minutes and drop in the chips.

The biggest distinction between Philips and other food processors is that it comes with a food divider, a basket and a cooking container. As a result, it's better suited for your kitchen.

Let's say you want to make different dishes such as brownies, quiches and jacket potatoes, all of which are dishes you could not do with the Tefal. It is easier to make curries in the Philips but not impossible.
This has merely outlined the basic information on air fryers and based on this information, and it has been determined that cooking potato chips in a low-fat air fryer do not yield chips that taste exactly like deep-fried chips. One could also conclude that since these are the closest you can get and are certainly healthier, they are most likely the product of your efforts.

CHAPTER 5
Consider Using Philips Airfryer

The Philips Airfryer uses air instead of oil to cook items such as French fries. I like eating fried meals but it doesn't mean everyone else does. I dislike the long-term damage that I'm always causing, such as weight gain, digestion difficulties and pimples, along with the oil that pours out of my pores.

As far as fried foods are concerned, I believe everyone should be free to enjoy French fries, fried chicken, and other fried meals without worrying about its consequences. However, Philips has, because of this new cooking technique, produced a cutting-edge breakthrough. The Airfryer has various qualities that make it worthwhile to own.

This modern-day deep fryer uses no oil to prepare fried dishes. It means that, out of all the things you cook in it, only 20% of the fat is left. Because it has no impact on weight or a person's overall diet, there is no reason to be concerned about weight gain or other harmful habits.

Additionally, the Airfryer comes with various amazing attachments that further elevate it to the industry's top. A divider for cooking multiple food types in one pan at the same time is known as a "food separator."

The divider is useful because it helps prevent the meals from mingling, so you don't have to worry about a certain sort of food tasting like another. That's terrible! My fries always tasted like chicken and now I won't be able to have that again.

Additionally, a unique air filter is included with this phone. Your home will no longer smell like food once you install this air filter, which will filter out the odors and vapors that generally fill your house when you are cooking in oil. You will not have to worry about the odor of fried meals or cooking oil lingering in your kitchen for many hours after you cook.

Flexibility: The timer may be set for up to 30 minutes and parents or those who need to multitask can utilize it. The timer will go off once the meal is ready to eat, which will produce a "ready" signal that lets you know it is time to eat. In this day and age, everyone should own a stylus.

The Philips Airfryer is a worthwhile investment for everyone who wishes to live healthily and prepare their food faster and more conveniently. This item is just amazing. If you've had it up to here with frying your dishes in oil and dealing with all of the after-effects, then you should check it out.

To achieve 80% less fat, you'll be able to fry meals without using any cooking oil and eat them with significantly less saturated fat. Not only will you be able to use all of the accessories that come with it but you will also use those accessories to make your life easier.

The fryer uses warm air to impact the food in a basket directly. Food placed in the basket slides into the device through a slot found at the front of the appliance, so it is unnecessary to lower food into boiling oil.

You use a simple thermostat to control the cooking temperature and a rotating timer to clock the cooking. The fryer switches itself off at the end of the cooking process. Instead of cooking many foods in one dish, simply use the basket divider.

Fried meals can be cooked successfully with no exception. Brownies and cakes can be cooked in the Airfryer too. This emphasizes the machine's adaptability. This is like a convection oven but with a basket used to keep it from deep-frying food.

But it's almost certainly correct to suggest that chips and/or fries will be the main part of most purchasers' cuisine. For these air fries, the Airfryer is especially useful.

You can use the machine as long as you take the time to investigate the types of potatoes to use, the ideal cooking time and the like. Remember that you will need to add roughly half a spoonful of oil each time you use it. The cooking time varies between 15–25 minutes according to the amount used and it is comparable to deep-frying or baking in the oven.

This is a space-saving food processor and it looks quite futuristic. It's easy to keep clean because all the parts that come into contact with the food are dishwasher safe. Additionally, there includes a quick start guide and a comprehensive recipe book with 30 different recipes for you to try.

It is quite obvious that the Philips Airfryer delivers as promised. Because of how good it is for your health, the health benefits of cooking with less fat cannot be refuted. With this multifunction fryer, you'll be able to do both and creating delicious cuisine.

CHAPTER 6

Tips For Making Healthier Fried Food Using Air Fryer

Many people find comfort in fried food, making it their favorite comfort meal. Every food lover has at least one guilty pleasure, whether French fries, cheese sticks or fried chicken. Frying food doesn't necessarily make it taste better, but it can decrease the dish's nutritional content if it's not cooked properly.

If you want to eat healthy while also enjoying fried food, there are a few tips to follow.

Use the Extra-Virgin Olive Oil

You should use olive oil for cooking when you are frying food since it is the greatest cooking oil. It has many health benefits. Thus it is better than the competition. Olive oil is more stable at high temperatures than sunflower, soybean and corn oil, making it suitable for cooking for a longer period. When buying olive oil, the only type of olive oil that you should purchase is virgin or extra virgin.

Make sure your oil is always clean

It is quite critical that you keep the oil you use for frying pleasant and clean. Once the oil becomes old and oxidized, it starts to burn and the food cooked in it will likewise taste burned.

As long as you're not a tightwad and are using up your old oil, no nutrition is there, so don't be stingy and change your oil quickly after noticing other cooked food residue in it. It is ideal for changing the oil after every three to four days, although it is advisable to conserve the old oil if you want to make greater use of it.

Take your batter to the next level

It is crucial to have a great batter while preparing fried food. However, the question is how the batter will determine if your food will be oily or healthful. In many recipes, individuals utilize all-purpose flour as a batter ingredient.

Also helpful are all-purpose flours, which contain gluten, which helps them adhere to the food, although they can absorb much oil. Use items that are naturally gluten-free, such as rice flour or cornmeal instead of all-purpose flour.
Baking soda or carbonated liquid may be used to aid your baking.

It is also possible to use baking soda or carbonated liquid to improve the quality of fried battered items. Because it releases gas bubbles when cooking, it assists food by preventing it from absorbing many oil.

Keep the oil at a steady temperature

Many people make the error of not maintaining the temperature of the oil when creating a healthy fried dish. Fry food oil should be heated to somewhere between 350°F and 400°F to get an optimal consistency.

Your meal will absorb more oil if the frying oil is not hot enough. If you fry the oil any hotter, it will burn and create smoke, which will result in terrible-tasting food and, even worse, poses a significant safety risk.

Also, keep in mind to use the best air fryer instead of woks or pans. With this change, you'll be able to keep the oil temperature and quality stable while also decreasing the danger. Fried meals don't have to be unhealthful. It is just a matter of knowing how to prepare them so they are good for you.

STRAWBERRY RHUBARB PARFAIT

Prep & Cook Time: 30 minutes | Servings: 1

INGREDIENTS

- 1 packet of plain full-fat yogurt (8.5 oz.)
- 2 tbsp. of toasted flakes
- 2 tbsp. of toasted coconut flakes
- 6 tbsp. of strawberry & rhubarb jam

INSTRUCTIONS

1. Add the jam into a dessert bowl (3 tbsp. per serving).
2. Add the crème fraîche & garnish with the toasted & coconut flakes.
3. Place inside your Air fryer and flash fry for a few seconds on a very high heat at 400°F/200°C (maximum possible), until the dessert is crisp on the outside and soft on the inside.
4. Serve!

SAUSAGE EGG MUFFINS

Prep & Cook Time: 30 minutes | Servings: 4

INGREDIENTS

- 6 oz. of Italian sausage
- 6 eggs
- 1/8 cup of heavy cream
- 3 oz. of cheese

INSTRUCTIONS

1. Preheat the Air Fryer to 350°F/175°C.
2. Grease a muffin pan.
3. Slice the sausage links & place them two to a tin.
4. Beat the eggs with the cream & season with salt & pepper.
5. Pour over the sausages in the tin.
6. Sprinkle with cheese & the remaining egg mixture.
7. Cook for 20 minutes or until the eggs are done & serve!

SALMON OMELET

Prep & Cook Time: 15 minutes | Servings: 2

INGREDIENTS

- 3 eggs
- 1 smoked salmon
- 3 links of pork sausage
- 1 cup of onions
- 1 cup of provolone cheese

INSTRUCTIONS

1. Whisk the eggs & pour them into a bowl. Place the bowl inside your Air Fryer's frying basket.
2. Cook briefly at 400°F/200°C for a few minutes each side.
3. Toss in the onions, salmon & cheese before turning the omelet over. Cook for a few more minutes.
4. Sprinkle the omelet with cheese & serve with the sausages on the side.
5. Serve!

BLACK'S BANGIN' CASSEROLE

Prep & Cook Time: 40 minutes | Servings: 4

INGREDIENTS

- 5 eggs
- 3 tbsp. of chunky tomato sauce
- 2 tbsp. of heavy cream
- 2 tbsp. of grated parmesan cheese

INSTRUCTIONS

1. Preheat your Air Fryer to 350°F/175°C.
2. Combine the eggs & cream in a bowl.
3. Mix in the tomato sauce & add the cheese.
4. Spread into a glass baking dish & bake for 25-35 minutes.
5. Top with extra cheese.
6. Enjoy!

POSH SOUFFLÉ

Prep & Cook Time: 25 minutes | Servings: 4

INGREDIENTS

- 1 cup of flour ⅓ cup of butter 1 cup of milk 4 egg yolks
- 1 tsp. of vanilla extract
- 6 egg whites
- 1 oz. of sugar
- 1 tsp. of cream of tartar

INSTRUCTIONS

1. Set your Air Fryer at 320°F & allow to warm.
2. In a bowl, mix together the butter & flour until a smooth consistency is achieved.
3. Pour the milk into a saucepan over a low-to-medium heat. Add in the & allow to dissolve before raising the heat to boil the milk.
4. Pour in the flour & butter mixture & stir rigorously for 7 minutes to eliminate any lumps. Make sure the mixture thickens. Take off the heat & allow to cool for 15 minutes.
5. Spritz 6 soufflé dishes with oil spray.
6. Place the egg yolks & vanilla extract in a separate bowl & beat them together with a fork. Pour in the milk & combine well to incorporate everything.
7. In a smaller bowl mix together the egg whites & cream of tartar with a fork. Fold into the egg yolks-milk mixture before adding in the flour

mixture. Transfer equal amounts to the 6 soufflé dishes.

8. Put the dishes in the Air Fryer & cook for 15 minutes.

EGG MUFFIN SANDWICH

Prep & Cook Time: 15 minutes | Servings: 1

INGREDIENTS

- 1 egg
- 2 slices of bacon
- 1 English muffin

INSTRUCTIONS

1. Pre-heat your Air Fryer at 395°F
2. Take a ramekin & spritz it with cooking spray. Break an egg into the ramekin before transferring it to the basket of your Air Fryer, along with the English muffin & bacon slices, keeping each component separate.
3. Allow to cook for 6 minutes. After removing from the Air Fryer, allow to cool for around two minutes. Halve the muffin.
4. Create your sandwich by arranging the egg & bacon slices on the base & topping with the other half of the muffin.

PEA DELIGHT

Prep & Cook Time: 25 minutes | Servings: 2 – 4

INGREDIENTS

- 1 cup of flour
- 1 tsp. of baking powder
- 3 eggs
- 1 cup of coconut milk
- 1 cup of cream cheese
- 3 tbsp. of pea protein
- 1 cup chicken/turkey strips
- 1 pinch sea salt
- 1 cup of mozzarella cheese

INSTRUCTIONS

1. Set your Air Fryer at 390°F & allow to warm.
2. In a large bowl, mix all ingredients together using a large wooden spoon.
3. Spoon equal amounts of the mixture into muffin cups & allow to cook for 15 minutes.

CHOCO BARS

Prep & Cook Time: 30 minutes | Servings: 8

INGREDIENTS

- 2 cups of old-fashioned oats
- 1 cup of quinoa, cooked
- 1 cup of chia seeds
- 1 cup almonds, sliced
- 1 cup of dried cherries, chopped
- 1 cup of dark chocolate, chopped ¾ cup of butter
- ⅓ cup of honey
- 2 tbsp. of coconut oil ¼ tsp. of salt
- cup of prunes, pureed

INSTRUCTIONS

1. Pre-heat your Air Fryer at 375°F.
2. Put the oats, quinoa, almonds, cherries, chia seeds, & chocolate in a bowl & mix well.
3. Heat the butter, honey, & coconut oil in a saucepan, gently stirring together. Pour this over the oat mixture.
4. Mix in the salt & pureed prunes & combine well.
5. Transfer this to a baking dish small enough to fit inside the Air Fryer & cook for 15 minutes. Remove from the Air Fryer & allow to cool completely. Cut into bars & enjoy.

FRENCH TOAST

Prep & Cook Time: 25 minutes | Servings: 2

INGREDIENTS

- 4 slices of bread of your choosing
- 2 tbsp. of soft butter
- 2 eggs, lightly beaten
- Salt
- Pinch of cinnamon
- Pinch of ground nutmeg
- Pinch of ground cloves
- Non-stick cooking spray
- Sugar for serving

INSTRUCTIONS

1. In a shallow bowl, mix together the salt, spices & eggs.
2. Butter each side of the slices of bread & slice into strips. You may also use cookie cutters for this step.
3. Set your Air Fryer to 350°F & allow to warm up briefly.
4. Dredge each strip of bread in the egg & transfer to the Air Fryer. Cook for two minutes, ensuring the toast turns golden brown.
5. At this point, spritz the tops of the bread strips with cooking spray, flip, & cook for another 4 minutes on the other side. Top with a light dusting of sugar before serving.

HASH BROWN

Prep & Cook Time: 20 minutes | Servings: 2

INGREDIENTS

- 12 oz. grated fresh cauliflower (about ½ a medium-sized head)
- 4 slices of bacon, chopped
- 3 oz. of onion, chopped
- 1 tbsp. of butter, softened

INSTRUCTIONS

1. In a skillet, sauté the bacon & onion until brown.
2. Add in the cauliflower & stir until tender & browned.
3. Add the butter steadily as it cooks.
4. Season to taste with salt & pepper.
5. Enjoy!

Sugary Oatmeal Muffins

Prep time: 10 minutes

Cooking time: 10 minutes

Servings: 2

INGREDIENTS:

- ¼ cup butter
- ¼ cup powdered sugar
- 2 eggs
- 1 tablespoon flour
- 1 pinch salt
- 2 tablespoon oatmeal
- 1 teaspoon vanilla extract

DIRECTIONS:

1. Melt the butter gently and combine it with the powdered sugar.
2. Start to mix the mixture using the hand mixer.
3. Beat the eggs in the separate bowl and whisk them until smooth.
4. When the butter mixture is smooth – start to add the eggs gradually.
5. Mix the butter mixture for 1 minute on the medium speed.
6. Then combine the flour and oatmeal together.
7. Add salt and stir it.
8. Add the flour mixture to the butter mixture.
9. After this, sprinkle it with the vanilla extract.
10. Knead the smooth and soft dough.

11. Preheat the air fryer to 360 F.
12. Place the dough into the muffin forms and place them in the air fryer.
13. Cook the muffins for 10 minutes.
14. Check if the muffins are cooked with the help of the
15. toothpick.
16. Serve the muffins warm!

Nutrition: calories 364, fat 27.8, fiber 0.6, carbs 22, protein 6.9

Tofu Potato Scramble

Prep time: 15 minutes

Cooking time: 13 minutes

Servings: 2

INGREDIENTS:

- 5 oz tofu
- 1 sweet potato
- ½ teaspoon canola oil
- 1 teaspoon soy sauce
- ¼ teaspoon garlic powder
- 1 teaspoon olive oil
- ½ teaspoon paprika
- ½ teaspoon dried oregano

DIRECTIONS:

1. Cut tofu into the cubes.
2. Sprinkle tofu cubes with the canola oil and soy sauce.
3. Add garlic powder and shake tofu gently.
4. Leave tofu for 10 minutes to marinate.
5. Meanwhile, peel the sweet potato and cut it into the same cubes as tofu.
6. Sprinkle the sweet potato with the olive oil, paprika, and dried oregano,
7. Mix it up.
8. Preheat the air fryer to 400 F.
9. Put the sweet potato in the air fryer basket and cook for 8 minutes.

10. After this, add marinated tofu and cook the meal for 5 minutes more.
11. When the meal is cooked – shake it well.
12. Then transfer to the serving plates.
13. Enjoy!

Nutrition: calories 137, fat 6.7, fiber 3, carbs 14, protein 7.3

Cinnamon French Toast

Prep time: 12 minutes

Cooking time: 10 minutes

Servings: 2

Ingredients:

- 2 egg
- 4 slices white bread
- 1 tablespoon sugar
- ¼ teaspoon cinnamon
- ¼ teaspoon ground ginger
- ¼ teaspoon ground nutmeg
- 1 teaspoon vanilla extract
- 2 tablespoon milk
- 1 tablespoon maple syrup

Directions:

1. Crack the eggs into the bowl and whisk them well.
2. Then sprinkle the whisked eggs with the cinnamon, ground ginger, ground nutmeg, and vanilla extract.
3. Add milk and sugar.
4. Whisk the mixture until sugar is dissolved.
5. After this, place the bread slices in the egg mixture and leave them until they soak all the egg liquid.
6. Preheat the air fryer to 355 F.

7. Put the bread slices on the rack and cook for 10 minutes.
8. When the toasts are cooked – serve them immediately.
9. Enjoy!

Nutrition: calories 176, fat 5.4, fiber 23.7, carbs 10.8, protein 7.5

Vanilla Bread Pudding

Prep time: 15 minutes

Cooking time: 22 minutes

Servings: 2

Ingredients:

- 4 white sandwich bread slices
- 1 egg
- ¼ cup heavy cream
- 1 teaspoon vanilla extract

- 3 teaspoon butter
- ½ teaspoon ground cinnamon
- 1 tablespoon almond flakes
- 2 teaspoon raisins
- ½ teaspoon olive oil

Directions:

1. Take off the crust from the sandwich bread slices.
2. Then spread every bread slice with the butter.
3. Spray the ramekin with the olive oil.
4. Place the first bread slice in the ramekin.
5. Then sprinkle it with the vanilla extract.
6. After this, the second bread slice in the ramekin and sprinkle it with the ground cinnamon.
7. Add the third bread slice and sprinkle it with the raisins.
8. Then put the last bread slice in the ramekin.
9. Crack the egg into the bowl and whisk it.
10. Add heavy cream and whisk it.
11. Pour the egg mixture into the ramekin.
12. Sprinkle the pudding mixture with the raisins.
13. Preheat the air fryer to 360 F.
14. Put the ramekin in the air fryer and cook it for 22
15. minutes.
16. Serve the cooked pudding immediately.
17. Enjoy!

Nutrition: calories 300, fat 16.7, fiber 0.4, carbs 31.7, protein 7.3

Mozzarella Sausage Stromboli

Prep time: 10 minutes

Cooking time: 10 minutes

Servings: 2

Ingredients:

- 4 oz pizza crust
- 3 oz mozzarella, shredded
- 3 oz sausages, cooked, sliced
- 1 egg yolk
- ¼ teaspoon cream
- 1 teaspoon oregano

Directions:

1. Roll the pizza crust.
2. Sprinkle the pizza crust with shredded mozzarella.
3. Then add the sliced sausages and sprinkle with the oregano.
4. Roll the pizza crust and secure it in the shape of the crescent.
5. Whisk the egg yolk well and combine it with the cream. Stir it.
6. Then brush the Stromboli with the egg yolk mixture.
7. Preheat the air fryer to 370 F.
8. Put the Stromboli in the air fryer basket and cook it for 10 minutes.
9. When the Stromboli is cooked – slice it.

Nutrition: calories 433, fat 23.7, fiber 1.2, carbs 29.4, protein 26.1

Cheese Popcorn

Cooking Time: 30 minutes

Yield: 4 servings

Ingredients

- 2 cups of halloumi, cut into ½-inch cubes
- 1 ¼ cups of panko bread crumbs
- 2 eggs
- 2 teaspoons of smoked paprika
- 1 teaspoon of cornflour
- 1 teaspoon of brown sugar
- 1 teaspoon of onion powder
- 1 teaspoon of mustard powder
- ½ teaspoon of garlic powder
- 1 teaspoon of chopped fresh thyme
- For Hot Maple Sauce:
- 1 ½ teaspoons of apple cider vinegar
- 1 tablespoon of sriracha chili sauce
- 1 tablespoon of maple syrup

Instructions

1. Add mustard powder, paprika, cornflour, sugar, garlic powder, and onion powder in a shallow dish. Mix it well until fully combined. Whisk eggs in a separate shallow dish. Mix the thyme with bread crumbs in a third shallow dish.
2. First, coat halloumi cubes with the seasoning mixture, then dip in

3. the whisked eggs and finally coat fully with the bread crumbs mixture. Place in the tray and put in the freezer for 5 minutes.
4. Meantime, prepare the Hot Maple Sauce. Pour the vinegar, chili sauce, and maple syrup into a small bowl and whisk until combined.
5. Preheat your air fryer to 180ºF. Cover the inside of the air fryer basket with baking paper.
6. Put the coated halloumi cubes in the preheated air fryer in a single layer. Avoid them touching! Cook at 180ºF for 6–8 minutes until the crust is golden. Remove and put on a serving plate. Repeat this step with the remaining part of the halloumi pieces.

Serve with Hot Maple Sauce and enjoy your Cheese Popcorn!

Nutrition Facts for 1 Serving, Calories: 375, Carbohydrates: 29.7 g, Fat: 19.8 g, Protein: 20.4 g,

Sugar: 6 g, Sodium: 1,003 mg, Cholesterol: 125 mg

Quick Bagels

Cooking Time: 30 minutes

Yield: 8 bagels

Ingredients

- 2 cups of unbleached all-purpose flour
- 2 cups of nonfat Greek yogurt
- 1 egg
- 1 tablespoon of baking powder
- 1 teaspoon of kosher salt
- Sesame seeds, bagel seasoning, poppy seeds, and/or shredded
- cheddar, for topping

Instructions

1. Add the flour, salt, and baking powder to a medium bowl. Stir to combine.
2. Pour in the Greek yogurt, continue stirring until fully combined. Form a dough ball. Spread some flour on the workplace and transfer the dough onto it.
3. Divide the formed dough into 8 even parts. Roll each part into a 9–10-inch rope and attach edges to make a bagel shape. Top each bagel with the whisked egg and your favorite toppings.
4. Preheat your air fryer to 350ºF. Spray the inside of the basket with some oil.
5. Put the prepared bagels in the preheated air fryer in a single layer. Avoid them touching! Cook at 350ºF for 10–12 minutes until golden.

Repeat the last part with the remaining part of the dough.

6. Let it cool for 5 minutes before serving. Enjoy your Quick Bagels!

Nutrition Facts for 1 Bagel, Calories: 166, Carbohydrates: 27 g, Fat: 2 g, Protein: 10 g, Sugar: 2 g, Sodium: 324 mg, Cholesterol: 24 mg

Onion Rings

Cooking Time: 30 minutes

Yield: 2 servings

Ingredients

- 1 large sweet onion, sliced in ½-inch-thick rings
- 1 cup of panko bread crumbs
- ½ cup of all-purpose flour
- ½ cup of buttermilk
- 1 egg
- 1 teaspoon of salt
- 1 teaspoon of paprika
- 2 tablespoons of olive oil

Instructions

1. Mix the paprika, flour, and ½ teaspoon of salt in a shallow bowl.
2. Whisk the egg, buttermilk, and ¼ cup of the flour mixture (from the first bowl) in a second shallow bowl. Combine the bread crumbs, olive oil, and ½ teaspoon of salt. Divide this mixture into 2 shallow bowls, so you can use the second part when the first one will become sticky.
3. Dry the onion rings with a paper towel. Using a fork, put the onion rings in the flour mixture, then dip in the egg-buttermilk mixture, and lastly, coat with the panko mixture.
4. Preheat your air fryer to 400ºF. Spray the inside of the basket with some oil.

5. Put the prepared onion rings in the air fryer in a single layer. You can put smaller rings inside the bigger ones; be sure to leave some space between each other.
6. Cook at 400°F for 11–15 minutes until golden crispy. Spray some oil over the tops after 6–7 minutes. Place on a serving plate. Repeat the last 2 steps with the remaining part of the onion rings.
7. Serve with your favorite sauce. Enjoy your Onion Rings!

Nutrition Facts for 1 Serving, Calories: 193, Carbohydrates: 26 g, Fat: 8 g, Protein: 4 g, Sugar: 9 g, Sodium: 1,208 mg, Cholesterol: 3 mg

Potato Wedges

Cooking Time: 30 minutes

Yield: 2 servings

Ingredients

- 1 russet potato
- ¼ cup of ketchup
- 1 tablespoon of chopped rosemary
- 1 tablespoon of olive oil
- ¼ teaspoon of smoked paprika
- Pinch of black pepper and salt, to taste

Instructions

1. Preheat your air fryer to 350ºF. Spray the inside of the basket with some oil.
2. Cut potato in half lengthwise, then slice each half in quarters. After that, cut each quarter into ¼-inch-thick wedge slices.
3. Transfer the potato slices to a bowl. Add in pepper, salt, rosemary, and olive oil. Toss them until fully coated.
4. Put in the preheated air fryer basket in a single layer. Cook at 350ºF for 17–20 minutes. Top with sea salt.
5. Whisk the ketchup with smoked paprika for extra flavor. Put in a serving bowl.
6. Serve with smoked ketchup. Enjoy your Potato Wedges!

Nutrition Facts for 1 Serving, Calories: 149, Carbohydrates: 19 g, Fat: 7 g, Protein: 2 g, Sugar: 1 g, Sodium: 160 mg

Garlic Bread Rolls

Cooking Time: 35 minutes

Yield: 4 servings

Ingredients

- 1 ½ cups of all-purpose flour
- 1/3 cup of butter
- 1 cup of milk
- 1 whisked egg
- 1 teaspoon of nutritional yeast
- 4 minced garlic cloves
- 1 tablespoon of fresh parsley
- 1 tablespoon of coconut oil
- 1 tablespoon of olive oil
- Pinch of black pepper and salt, to taste

Instructions

1. Rub the butter into the flour until fully mixed in. Warm oil and milk in the pot on low heat until lightly warm. Transfer the milk- oil mixture into the bowl and add the nutritional yeast. Mix the ingredients with your hands until you make a dough.
2. Knead the prepared dough for about 5 minutes. Transfer the dough into the air fryer basket. Let it prove at 140ºF for 10 minutes.
3. Remove and form equal medium-sized bread rolls.
4. Place the formed bread rolls into the air fryer, touching each other.

5. Cook at 365ºF for 15 minutes. Open the air fryer before 5 minutes from the final time and brush the rolls with the whisked egg mixture.
6. Remove from the air fryer. Spread the minced garlic with parsley over the tops.
7. Serve and enjoy your Garlic Bread Rolls!

Nutrition Facts for 1 Serving, Calories: 652, Carbohydrates: 90 g, Fat: 26 g, Protein: 15 g, Sugar: 4 g, Sodium: 167 mg, Cholesterol: 47 mg

Crispy Chickpeas

Cooking Time: 1 hour 20 minutes

Yield: 2 cups

Ingredients

- 1 can (16 ounces) of chickpeas
- ½ teaspoon of salt
- ¼ teaspoon of smoked paprika
- ¼ teaspoon of garlic powder
- ¼ teaspoon of onion powder
- 1/8 teaspoon of ground black pepper

Instructions

1. Drain and rinse chickpeas. First, dry them with a paper towel, and then put chickpeas in the air fryer for 5 minutes to quickly dry.
2. Put the chickpeas, paprika, oil, paprika, garlic powder, onion powder, black pepper, and salt in a medium bowl. Toss them until fully coated.
3. Put the prepared chickpeas in the air fryer in a single layer, spreading through the bottom of the basket. Cook at 365ºF for 12 minutes, stirring 2–3 times for evenly cooking.
4. Serve with your favorite sauce. Enjoy your Crispy Chickpeas!

Nutrition Facts for 1 Serving (½ Cup), Calories: 32, Carbohydrates: 0 g, Fat: 3 g, Protein: 0 g,

Sodium: 265 mg

GRILLED HAM & CHEESE
Prep & Cook Time: 30 minutes | Servings: 2

INGREDIENTS

- 3 buns
- 4 slices of medium-cut deli ham
- 1 tbsp. of salted butter
- 1 oz. of flour
- 3 slices of cheddar cheese
- 3 slices of muenster cheese

INSTRUCTIONS

Bread:

1. Preheat your Air Fryer to 350°F/175°C.
2. Mix the flour, salt & baking powder in a bowl. Put to the side.
3. Add in the butter & coconut oil to a skillet.
4. Melt for 20 seconds & pour into another bowl.
5. In this bowl, mix in the dough.
6. Scramble two eggs. Add to the dough.
7. Add ½ tbsp. of coconut flour to thicken, & place evenly into a cupcake tray. Fill about ¾ inch.
8. Bake for 20 minutes until browned.
9. Allow to cool for 15 minutes & cut each in half for the buns.

Sandwich:

1. Fry the deli meat in a skillet on a high heat.
2. Put the ham & cheese between the buns.

3. Heat the butter on medium high.
4. When brown, turn to low & add the dough to pan.
5. Press down with a weight until you smell burning, then flip to crisp both sides.
6. Enjoy!

MELTED PROSCIUTTO SPINACH SALAD

Prep & Cook Time: 5 minutes | Servings: 2

INGREDIENTS

- 2 cups of baby spinach
- lb. of prosciutto
- 1 cantaloupe
- 1 avocado
- ¼ cup of diced red onion handful of raw, of walnuts

INSTRUCTIONS

1. Put a cup of spinach on each plate.
2. Top with the diced prosciutto, cubes of balls of melon, slices of avocado, a handful of red onion & a few walnuts.
3. Add some freshly ground pepper, if you like.
4. Flash fry inside your Air Fryer at 400°F/200°C until the salad is crisp.
5. Serve!

RICED CAULIFLOWER & CURRY CHICKEN

Prep & Cook Time: 40 minutes | Servings: 6

INGREDIENTS

- 2 lb. of chicken (4 breasts)
- 1 packet of curry paste
- 3 tbsp. of butter
- ½ cup of heavy cream
- 1 head cauliflower (around 1 kg)

INSTRUCTIONS

1. Add the curry paste and chicken to a dish. Mix. Place inside your Air Fryer and cook at 400°F/200°C for 25 minutes.
2. Cut a cauliflower head into florets & blend in a food processor to make the riced cauliflower.
3. When the chicken is cooked, uncover, add the cream & cook for an additional 7 minutes.
4. Serve!

MASHED GARLIC TURNIPS

Prep & Cook Time: 10 minutes | Servings: 2

INGREDIENTS

- 3 cups of diced turnip
- 2 cloves of garlic, minced
- 1 cup of heavy cream
- 3 tbsp. of melted butter Salt & pepper to season

INSTRUCTIONS

1. Fry the turnips inside your Air Fryer at 400°F/200°C until tender.
2. Drain & mash the turnips.
3. Add the cream, butter, salt, pepper & garlic. Combine well.
4. Serve!

LASAGNA SPAGHETTI SQUASH

Prep & Cook Time: 90 minutes | Servings: 6

INGREDIENTS

- 25 slices of mozzarella cheese
- 1 jar (40 oz.) of Marinara sauce
- 30 oz. of whole-milk ricotta cheese
- 2 large spaghetti squash, cooked (44 oz.)
- 4 lb. of ground beef

INSTRUCTIONS

1. Preheat your Air Fryer to 375°F/190°C.
2. Slice the spaghetti squash & place it face down inside a Air Fryer proof dish. Fill with water until covered.
3. Bake for 45 minutes until skin is soft.
4. Sear the meat until browned.
5. In a large skillet, heat the browned meat & marinara sauce. Set aside when warm.
6. Scrape the flesh off the cooked squash to resemble strands of spaghetti.
7. Layer the lasagna in a large, greased pan in alternating layers of spaghetti squash, meat sauce, mozzarella, ricotta. Repeat until all increased have been used.
8. Bake for 30 minutes & serve!

BLUE CHEESE CHICKEN WEDGES

Prep & Cook Time: 45 minutes | Servings: 4

INGREDIENTS

- Blue cheese dressing
- 2 tbsp. of crumbled blue cheese
- 4 strips of bacon
- 2 chicken breasts (boneless)
- 1 cup of your favorite buffalo sauce

INSTRUCTIONS

1. Cook the chicken & buffalo sauce inside your Air Fryer at 400°F/200°C for 35 minutes.
2. Add the blue cheese & buffalo pulled chicken. Top with the cooked bacon crumble.
3. Serve & enjoy.

OH SO GOOD' SALAD

Prep & Cook Time: 10 minutes | Servings: 2

INGREDIENTS

- 6 brussels sprouts
- 1 tsp. of apple cider vinegar
- 1 tsp. of olive/grapeseed oil
- 1 grind of salt
- 1 tbsp. of freshly grated parmesan

INSTRUCTIONS

1. Slice the clean brussels sprouts in half.
2. Cut thin slices in the opposite direction.
3. Once sliced, cut the roots off & discard.
4. Toss together with the apple cider, oil & salt.
5. Sprinkle with the parmesan cheese.
6. Flash fry in your Air Fryer at 400°F/200°C for 23 minutes until the cheese is melted and crisp. Take out and let cool. Serve!

THYME LAMB RIBS

Prep time: 10 minutes

Cooking time: 30 minutes

Servings: 2

Ingredients

- 1 tablespoon flour
- 14 oz lamb ribs
- 1 egg
- 1 teaspoon thyme
- 1 teaspoon lemon juice
- 1 teaspoon cream
- 1 garlic clove, sliced
- 1 tablespoon canola oil
- 1 teaspoon rosemary
- ½ teaspoon paprika

Directions:

1. Sprinkle the lamb ribs with the thyme, lemon juice, cream, sliced garlic, canola oil, rosemary, and paprika.
2. Massage the lamb ribs gently.
3. Then crack the egg into the bowl and whisk it.
4. Dip the lamb ribs in the whisked egg.
5. After this, sprinkle the meat with the flour.
6. Preheat the air fryer to 345 F and put the lamb ribs in the air fryer basket.
7. Cook the meal for 25 minutes.

8. After this, increase the temperature to 370 F and cook the lamb ribs for 5 minutes more.
9. Let the cooked lamb ribs chill gently.
10.   Enjoy!

Nutrition: calories 577, fat 36, fiber 0.8, carbs 4.8, protein 55.4

CURRY CHICKEN BREAST

Prep time: 20 minutes

Cooking time: 10 minutes

Servings: 2

Ingredients

- 15 oz chicken breast
- 1 tablespoon turmeric
- 1 teaspoon curry paste
- ½ yellow onion, diced
- 1 tablespoon mayonnaise
- ½ teaspoon onion powder
- ½ teaspoon garlic powder
- 1 teaspoon butter

Directions:

1. Combine together turmeric, curry paste, sided onion, mayonnaise, onion powder, and garlic powder.
2. Churn the mixture well.
3. Melt the butter and add churned mixture. Stir it.
4. After this, brush the chicken breast with the turmeric mixture and leave it for 10 minutes.
5. Preheat the air fryer to 380 F.
6. Put the chicken breast in the air fryer basket and cook for 10 minutes.
7. Flip the chicken breast into another side after 5 minutes of cooking.
8. Serve the cooked chicken breast immediately.
9. Enjoy!

Nutrition: calories 332, fat 11.5, fiber 1.4, carbs 8.2, protein 46.1

Maple Turkey Breast

Prep time: 10 minutes

Cooking time: 35 minutes

Servings: 2

Ingredients

- 1 teaspoon canola oil
- 1 teaspoon ground coriander
- ½ teaspoon turmeric
- ½ teaspoon onion powder
- ½ teaspoon oregano
- ½ teaspoon salt
- 1 teaspoon Dijon mustard
- 2 tablespoon maple syrup
- 1 tablespoon butter
- 14 oz turkey breast

Directions:

1. Combine the canola oil, ground coriander, turmeric, onion powder, oregano, and salt.
2. Churn the mixture to make the spice oil.
3. Brush the turkey breast with the spicy oil.
4. Melt the butter and combine it with the maple syrup, and Dijon mustard. Whisk it.
5. Preheat the air fryer to 360 F and put the turkey breast in the air fryer basket.
6. Cook the turkey breast for 25 minutes.
7. When the time is over – flip the turkey breast to another side.

8. Sprinkle the turkey breast with the maple syrup mixture generously.
9. Cook the meal for 10 minutes at 355 F. Let the cooked turkey breast chill little. Slice it.
10.   Enjoy!

Nutrition: calories 337, fat 4.5, fiber 1.4, carbs 23, protein 34.2

Rosemary Salmon Steak

Prep time: 10 minutes

Cooking time: 12 minutes

Servings: 2

Ingredients

- 2 salmon steaks
- ½ teaspoon salt
- ½ teaspoon ground coriander
- ½ teaspoon dried rosemary
- 1 teaspoon onion powder
- 1 tablespoon olive oil

Directions:

1. Sprinkle the salmon steaks with the salt, ground coriander, dried rosemary, and onion powder.
2. Then sprinkle the salmon steaks with the olive oil.
3. Put the salmon steaks in the air fryer basket and cook them for 12 minutes at 265 F.
4. When the salmon steaks are cooked - serve them immediately.

Nutrition: calories 301, fat 18.1, fiber 0.2, carbs 1.2, protein 34.7

Stuffed Calamari

Prep time: 15 minutes

Cooking time: 10 minutes

Servings: 2

Ingredients:

- 2 calamari tubes
- 1 red sweet pepper
- 1 tablespoon fresh dill, chopped
- ½ teaspoon salt
- ½ teaspoon chili flakes
- ½ teaspoon turmeric
- 1 tablespoon olive oil
- 1 teaspoon garlic, sliced
- ½ teaspoon butter

Directions:

1. Preheat the air fryer to 400 F.
2. Put the red sweet pepper in the air fryer basket and cook it for 5 minutes.
3. Then remove the red sweet pepper from the air fryer basket tray and discard the seeds.
4. Chop the red sweet pepper and combine it with the chopped fresh dill.
5. Add sliced garlic and mix it.
6. After this, sprinkle the calamari tubes with the salt, chili flakes, turmeric, and olive oil.
7. Fill the calamari tubes with the red sweet pepper mixture and butter.
8. Secure the calamari tubes with the toothpicks.
9. Preheat the air fryer to 400 F.
10. Sprinkle the calamari tubes with the olive oil and put in the air fryer basket.
11. Cook the calamari tubes for 5 minutes.
12. When the meal is cooked – chill it little.

13. Serve it!

Nutrition: calories 192, fat 10, fiber 1.2, carbs 8.8, protein 16.1

Cream Cheese Baked Potato

Prep time: 15 minutes

Cooking time: 22 minutes

Servings: 2

Ingredients:

- 1 teaspoon cream cheese
- 2 potatoes
- ½ teaspoon salt
- ½ teaspoon white pepper
- ½ onion, sautéed
- 1 oz sweet peas, cooked
- 1 teaspoon butte
- ½ teaspoon minced garlic

Directions

1. Preheat the air fryer to 365 F.
2. Wash the potatoes carefully and place them in the air fryer basket.
3. Cook the potatoes for 18 minutes.
4. Meanwhile, churn together the cream cheese, minced garlic, and white pepper.
5. Add the sautéed onion and sweet peas.
6. Add salt and mix the mixture up.
7. After this, melt the butter.
8. When the time is over – remove the baked potatoes from the air fryer and cut them into the halves.

9. Scoop the flesh from the potatoes gently.
10. Combine the potato flesh and cream cheese mixture together.
11. Then fill the potato halves with the cream cheese mixture.
12. Put the potatoes in the air fryer.
13. Cook the meal for 4 minutes at 400 F.
14. When the potatoes are cooked – let them chill gently.
15. Enjoy!

Nutrition: calories 195, fat 2.8, fiber 6.6, carbs 38.7, protein 4.9

Cayenne Pepper Brussels Sprouts

Prep time: 10 minutes

Cooking time: 15 minutes

Servings: 2

Ingredients:

- 1 tablespoon butter
- 10 oz Brussel sprouts
- ½ teaspoon cayenne pepper
- 4 tablespoon chicken stock
- 1 teaspoon paprika
- ½ teaspoon lemon juice
- ¼ teaspoon salt

Directions:

1. Cut Brussel sprouts into the halves.
2. Churn the butter with the cayenne pepper and paprika.
3. Add salt and stir it carefully.
4. Then sprinkle Brussels sprouts halves with the lemon juice.
5. Preheat the air fryer to 380 F.
6. Put the butter mixture in the air fryer basket.
7. Melt the butter and add Brussel sprouts halves.
8. Cook the vegetables for 15 minutes. Shake the vegetables after 7 minutes of cooking.
9. Then let the cooked vegetables chill gently.
10. 10.Enjoy!

Nutrition: calories 118, fat 6.5, fiber 5.8, carbs 13.9, protein 5.2

Bell Pepper Slices

Prep time: 20 minutes

Cooking time: 10 minutes

Servings: 2

Ingredients:

- 1 sweet red pepper
- 1 yellow sweet pepper
- 1 garlic clove
- 1 tablespoon apple cider vinegar
- 1 teaspoon olive oil
- ½ teaspoon dried dill
- ½ teaspoon dried parsley
- 1 teaspoon butter
- 1 pinch salt

Directions:

1. Wash the sweet peppers carefully and discard seeds.
2. Slice the sweet peppers.
3. Preheat the air fryer to 400 F.
4. Toss the butter in the air fryer basket and melt it.
5. Then add the sweet peppers slices.
6. Cook the sweet peppers for 10 minutes.
7. Shake them well after 5 minutes of cooking.
8. Meanwhile, peel the garlic clove and slice it.
9. Combine the sliced garlic with the apple cider vinegar and olive oil.

10. Add dried dill and dried parsley.
11. Sprinkle the mixture with the pinch of salt and whisk it well.
12. When the peppers are cooked – let the chill till the room temperature.
13. Then sprinkle the sweet peppers with the oily mixture well.
14. Put the meal in the fridge for 10 minutes.
15. Serve it!

Nutrition: calories 86, fat 4.6, fiber 1.7, carbs 11.1, protein 1.7

Sugary Pumpkin Wedges

Prep time: 15 minutes

Cooking time: 8 minutes

Servings: 2

Ingredients:

- 1 teaspoon raisins
- 12 oz pumpkin
- 1 teaspoon ground cinnamon
- 1 teaspoon butter
- 5 tablespoon water
- 2 tablespoon brown sugar
- 1 teaspoon fresh ginger, grated

Directions:

1. Peel the pumpkin and cut it into the serving wedges.
2. Melt the butter and combine it together with the ground cinnamon, brown sugar, and grated ginger.
3. Churn the mixture gently.
4. Rub every pumpkin wedge with the butter mixture well. Leave it.
5. Preheat the air fryer to 390 F.
6. Pour water into the air fryer basket.
7. Add raisins and pumpkin wedges.
8. After this, add all the remaining juice from the pumpkin wedges.
9. Cook the pumpkin for 5 minutes.

10. After this, flip the pumpkin wedges into another
11. side.
12. Cook the pumpkin wedges for 3 minutes more.
13. Then transfer the cooked pumpkin wedges into the serving plates.
14. Sprinkle the pumpkin wedges with the raisins.
15. Enjoy!

Nutrition: calories 119, fat 2.5, fiber 5.7, carbs 25.4, protein 2.1

Cream Cheese Spinach

Prep time: 15 minutes

Cooking time: 10 minutes

Servings: 2

Ingredients:

- ¼ cup cream
- 1 tablespoon cream cheese
- 1cup spinach
- ½ onion, diced, boiled
- ½ teaspoon salt
- 1 teaspoon butter
- ½ teaspoon ground black pepper
- 2 bacon slices, cooked, chopped
- ½ teaspoon paprika

Directions:

1. Preheat the air fryer to 330 F.
2. Toss the butter in the air fryer basket and melt.
3. Meanwhile, chop the spinach and sprinkle it with the salt.
4. Let the spinach gives the juice.
5. When the butter is melted – put the spinach with the remaining juice in the air fryer basket.
6. Sprinkle the spinach with the cream cheese, cream, diced onion, ground black pepper, and paprika.
7. Stir the mixture gently with the help of the wooden spatula.

8. Cook the spinach for 5 minutes.
9. After this, stir the spinach gently and add chopped bacon.
10. Cook the spinach for 5 minutes more.
11. Then stir the cooked meal carefully.
12. Transfer the cooked spinach to the serving plates.
13. Serve it!

Nutrition: calories 174, fat 13.4, fiber 1.3, carbs 5.1, protein 8.6

Creamy Leek

Prep time: 10 minutes

Cooking time: 11 minutes

Servings: 2

Ingredients:

- ½ teaspoon baking soda
- 1 tablespoon sugar
- 11 oz leek
- 3 tablespoon cream

- ¼ teaspoon salt
- 1 tablespoon butter
- 3 tablespoon chicken stock
- ¼ teaspoon turmeric

Directions:

1. Chop the leek.
2. Preheat the air fryer to 390 F.
3. Toss the butter there and melt it.
4. Then add cream and chicken stock.
5. After this, add the chopped leek.
6. Sprinkle the leek with the sugar, salt, baking soda, and turmeric. Stir it carefully.
7. Cook the leek for 5 minutes.
8. After this, shake the leek carefully and cook for 6 minutes more.
9. When the leek is soft and light brown – it is cooked.
10. Let it chill for 3 minutes, Serve the meal.

Nutrition: calories 182, fat 7.3, fiber 2.9, carbs 28.9, protein 2.6

Garlic Brussels Sprouts

Cooking Time: 20 minutes

Yield: 4 servings

Ingredients

- 1 pound of trimmed brussels sprouts
- ½ cup of panko bread crumbs
- 1 ½ teaspoons of minced fresh rosemary
- 2 minced garlic cloves
- ½ teaspoon of salt
- ¼ teaspoon of black pepper
- 3 tablespoons of olive oil

Instructions

1. Preheat your air fryer to 350ºF. Spray some oil inside the air fryer basket.
2. Mix oil, garlic, salt, and pepper in a small bowl. Toss Brussels sprouts with 2 tablespoons of the prepared oil mixture. Transfer them into the preheated air fryer basket and cook at 350ºF for 8 minutes, stirring halfway, until lightly browned.
3. Mix rosemary, bread crumbs, and the remaining part of the oil mixture in a bowl. Sprinkle the prepared mixture over sprouts.
1. Continue cooking for extra 3–4 minutes until tender and crumbs are browned.
4. Serve warm and enjoy your Garlic Brussels Sprouts!

Nutrition Facts for 1 Serving (¾ Cup), Calories: 164, Carbohydrates: 15 g, Fat: 11 g, Protein: 5 g, Sugar: 3 g, Sodium: 342 mg

Roasted Green Beans

Cooking Time: 15 minutes

Yield: 6 servings

Ingredients

- 1 pound of fresh green beans
- ½ pound of sliced mushrooms
- 1 sliced small red onion
- 1 teaspoon of Italian seasonings
- ¼ teaspoon of salt
- 1/8 teaspoon of black pepper
- 2 tablespoons of olive oil

Instructions

1. Preheat your air fryer to 350ºF. Spray some oil inside the air fryer basket.
2. Mix all the ingredients in a bowl, toss them until fully coated.
3. Transfer the prepared mixture in the preheated air fryer basket.
5. Cook at 350ºF for 8–10 minutes until tender or 10–12 minutes until browned.
4. Serve warm and enjoy your Roasted Green Beans!

Nutrition Facts for 1 Serving (2/3 Cup), Calories: 76, Carbohydrates: 8 g, Fat: 5 g, Protein: 3 g, Sugar: 3 g, Sodium: 105 mg

Homemade French Fries

Cooking Time: 20 minutes- Yield: 4 servings

Ingredients

- 2-3 medium russet potatoes
- 1 tablespoon of Cajun seasoning
- Pinch of salt and black pepper, to taste
- 1 tablespoon of olive oil

Instructions

1. Preheat your air fryer to 375ºF. Spray some oil inside the air fryer basket.
2. Cut the washed potatoes into ¼-inch fries. Put them in a large bowl, add oil with seasonings and toss.
3. Transfer potatoes in the preheated air fryer basket. Cook at 375ºF for 12–15 minutes, shaking halfway, until crispy.
4. Serve with the preferred sauce and enjoy your Homemade French Fries!

Nutrition Facts for 1 Serving, Calories: 120, Carbohydrates: 20 g, Fat: 4 g, Protein: 3 g, Sugar: 1 g, Sodium: 7 mg

Zucchini Fries

Cooking Time: 15 minutes

Yield: 4 servings

Ingredients

- 2 medium zucchini
- ½ cup of grated Parmesan cheese
- ½ cup of almond flour or panko bread crumbs
- 1 large egg
- 1 teaspoon of Italian seasoning
- ½ teaspoon of garlic powder
- Pinch of black pepper and salt, to taste

Instructions

1. Preheat your air fryer to 400ºF. Spray some oil inside the air fryer basket.
2. Cut zucchini into ½-inch thick and 3–4 inches long.
3. Add almond flour (or bread crumbs), spices, Parmesan, salt, and pepper in a shallow bowl. Stir it until combined. Whisk the egg in a separate bowl.
4. Dip zucchini sticks in the egg mixture, then coat with the flour mixture. Transfer them in the preheated air fryer basket in a single layer and spray tops with olive oil. Cook at 400ºF for 10 minutes, shaking halfway, until crispy. Repeat the last step with the remaining part of zucchinis.
5. Serve with the preferred sauce and enjoy your Zucchini Fries!

Nutrition Facts for 1 Serving, Calories: 147, Carbohydrates: 6 g, Fat: 10 g, Protein: 9 g, Sugar: 3 g, Sodium: 224 mg, Cholesterol: 49 mg

CPSIA information can be obtained
at www.ICGtesting.com
Printed in the USA
BVHW050926150721
612039BV00012B/402